Usborne Spotter's Guides
WILD
ANIMALS

Rosamund Kidman Cox

Illustrated by Malcolm McGregor

Additional illustrations ... ... hris Lyon,
Rachel Lockwood, An ... ... nil Weare,
David Quinn, Chris ... ... Vright

Edited by Phillip Clarke and Clare Hickman
Designed by Karen Tomlins and Joanne Kirkby
Cover designer: Michael Hill
Series designer: Laura Fearn
Expert consultants: Margaret Rostron and
Sue Matthews (Zoological Society of London)

Acknowledgements: Cover © Digital Vision;
4–5 © Paul A. Souders/Corbis; 1–3, 6–9, 12–15, 18–19,
24–27, 30–31, 34–39, 44–49, 52–55 © Digital Vision.

This edition first published in 2006 by Usborne Publishing Ltd.,
Usborne House, 83-85 Saffron Hill, London, EC1N 8RT, England.
www.usborne.com

Printed in China

CONTENTS

HOW TO USE THIS BOOK

This book is an identification guide to some of the world's wild animals. A number of these creatures may be seen in the wild, but most people will probably see them only in wildlife parks or zoos.

Some people think that keeping animals in captivity is wrong. While it is true that there still are zoos that do not give animals the resources they need to be happy, many modern zoos help animal conservation by breeding creatures that are endangered in the wild. Some animals are now so rare that they can only be found in zoos.

The American bald eagle was nearly made extinct by hunting and pollution. Now it is thriving again due to conservation laws and breeding in zoos.

Throughout this book, you will find suggested links to wild animal websites. For a complete list of links and instructions, turn to pages 60 and 61.

Each animal pictured in this book has a description telling you about it, including its measurements, a little about the way it behaves and where it is from. A world map on page 59 shows all the areas mentioned in this book.

Sometimes both the male ♂ and female ♀ of a species are shown. If the sexes look alike, only one is shown and there is no symbol. There is also a small circle to tick when you have spotted an animal.

In this book, each type, or species, of animal shown is grouped with animals related to it. For example, all the big cats (such as lions and tigers) are found together.

There is a separate grouping for nocturnal animals (animals active mainly at night). Animals that are very rare in the wild are also grouped on the same pages.

This is an example of how the animals are shown in the book.

⬇ REEVES' MUNTJAC
Male has small antlers. Holds its head low when running. Barks when alarmed. China. SH 50cm.

Where the animal is found

Measurements (explained on next page)

♂—Sex symbol

Tick when animal is spotted ✔

USEFUL WORDS
On page 62 there is a list of words used to describe wild animals, with a short description of what each means.

5

MEASUREMENTS

Different types of animal are measured in different ways to give the most useful information. In this book, for birds and most reptiles, the total body length (TL), including the tail, is given. Reptiles with shells are measured by the length of their shell (SL).

Most mammals are measured by head and body length (H&B) only (not including the tail). For hoofed mammals, the shoulder height (SH) is given.

Measurements are usually given as averages, but some are the maximum size of the animal. This often means that one sex is very much larger than the other.

Total length (TL)

Shell length (SL)

Head and body length (H&B)

Shoulder height (SH)

Total length (TL)

WILDLIFE PARKS AND ZOOS

When visiting a zoo or wildlife park, remember that animals are generally most active in the early morning or late afternoon. It is also a good idea to contact the place you intend to visit to find out about any special events they may be holding.

When you arrive, buy a map to tell you where the different animals are. Also check the main noticeboard for details of feeding times and of any baby animals that may have been born.

Never feed the animals. They have their own special diets, and could be harmed by eating too much food or the wrong type of food.

VISITING SAFARI PARKS

If you are visiting a park where you have to travel around by car, remember to take some binoculars. This way you will be able to watch closely even nervous animals that keep their distance.

Hippos spend most of the day in the water, coming onto land to graze.

WATCHING ANIMALS

Wildlife parks and zoos are good places to study the way animals behave. You could look out for some of the features listed here.

• **Teeth** The shape and size of an animal's teeth can tell you a lot about what it eats. Look in the animal's enclosure for further clues to its diet.

• **Colour and size** With many animals, these can provide important clues to age and sex.

• **Special adaptations** The physical characteristics of animals often reveal their lifestyle. Many monkeys, for example, have tails that are specially adapted for grasping branches.

A lion's large canine teeth show that it is a carnivore (meat-eater).

For a link to an online encyclopedia of animals, turn to page 60.

• Sleeping position

A number of hoofed animals, for example the giraffe, sleep standing up.

• Group behaviour

Animals living in groups act differently according to their position in the group's social order. The leader of a grey wolf pack, for example, shows its importance by growling and raising its ears and tail. A more lowly wolf will flatten its ears and tuck its tail between its legs to show that it knows its place.

• Movement The way an

animal moves can yield clues to its lifestyle. A spider monkey's ability to swing, for example, tells of its life in the treetops.

Springboks are named for the agile leaping by which they escape danger.

LATIN NAMES

The sign on an animal's enclosure often shows a Latin name as well as a common name. Common names vary from place to place, but Latin names stay the same.

LION

Species: *Panthera leo*
Family: *Felidae*
Order: *Carnivora*

JUNGLE CAT

Species: *Felis chaus*
Family: *Felidae*
Order: *Carnivora*

Latin names show how animals are related. Both animals above, for example, belong to a large group, or order, called the *Carnivora* (Meat-eaters). Within this order, they both belong to the Cat family (*Felidae*). Within this family, the lion is a species, or type, among the Big Cats (*Panthera*), while the jungle cat is grouped with the Smaller Cats (*Felis*).

9

APES

➡ ORANG-UTAN
Strong but gentle.
Unlike other apes in
that it lives alone. It
prefers to sleep off
the ground. Rare.
Sumatra; Borneo.
H&B 1.4m.

⬅ LOWLAND GORILLA
Shy, gentle, intelligent
and very strong. Lives
in groups. Dominant
males are called
"silverbacks" because
of their colour. Rare.
Central W Africa.
H&B 1.5m.

Uses its front
knuckles when
walking

➡ CHIMPANZEE
Excitable. Adult chimps
can be dangerous.
Watch how they
communicate with
facial expressions.
Rare. Central W
Africa. H&B 1m.

10

For a link to a website with animal videos and games, turn to page 60.

GIBBON, MONKEYS

Can swing along very quickly using its long arms

➡ WHITE-HANDED GIBBON
Also called a **Lar Gibbon**. It lives in pairs with its young. Moves by swinging rather than climbing. Listen for its hooting call. Rare. S-E Asia. H&B 50cm.

➡ PIG-TAILED MACAQUE
Lives in large troops. Try to spot the dominant male leader: he often pouts as a threat or greeting. S-E Asia. H&B 60cm max.

♂

Flesh-coloured rump

⬅ GELADA
The female's chest patch only turns red at mating time. An angry male flashes white eyelids and exposes his canine teeth. Ethiopia. H&B 70cm max.

♂

⬅ MANDRILL
The male leader is the largest, and has the most brightly coloured face and rump. He sometimes barks. W Africa. H&B 80cm.

♂

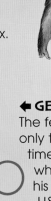

11

For a link to a website with fast facts about animals, turn to page 60.

MONKEYS

➡ VERVET MONKEY
In zoos, older same-
sex monkeys fight.
Young or parents
do not. Grooming
builds friendship.
Africa. H&B 60cm.

➡ PATAS MONKEY
You will see it on the
ground, but it sleeps in
branches. Females are very
possessive of their young.
C & S Africa. H&B 80cm.

♂

♂

⬅ ABYSSINIAN COLOBUS
Shy. Spends most of its
time in the trees. Babies
may be passed around
between the females.
Africa. H&B 65cm.

⬅ PROBOSCIS MONKEY
Nose grows throughout life.
The male's is longer than
the female's. If alarmed,
the male's nose straightens.
Rare. Borneo. H&B 75cm.

SOUTH AMERICAN MONKEYS

➡ SQUIRREL MONKEY
Lives in big groups. Runs along branches on all fours, using its tail as a balance. S America. H&B 35cm.

➡ HUMBOLDT'S WOOLLY MONKEY
Has a prehensile tail which can grip branches or even grasp bits of food. S America. H&B 70cm.

♂

⬅ WHITE-FACED SAKI
Easily frightened, it makes loud, bird-like alarm calls. The male helps carry the young. S America. H&B 50cm max.

➡ COMMON MARMOSET
In zoos, can only be kept in pairs. The male often carries the young. S America H&B 20cm.

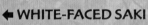

LEMURS, TREE-SHREW, SLOTH

➡ RUFFED LEMUR
Its fur may be a mixture of red, black and white. Makes loud, barking calls when upset. Rare. Madagascar. H&B 60cm.

➡ RING-TAILED LEMUR
May live in big groups. Females are dominant over males. Madagascar. H&B 40cm.

Two claws on front feet

⬅ COMMON TREE-SHREW
Fast mover. Young are left in a nest separate from the mother's. She tends them every few days. S-E Asia. H&B 20cm

⬅ TWO-TOED SLOTH
Sleeps, eats, mates and gives birth upside-down. A slow mover, and very slow on the ground. Eats mainly leaves. S America. H&B 60cm.

For a link to animal fact files with video and audio clips, turn to page 60.

GIANT ANTEATER, ELEPHANTS

➡ GIANT ANTEATER
Sleeps for most of the day, its tail curled around it. Has no teeth. Laps up termites with its long, sticky tongue. C & S America. H&B 1m.

⬇ INDIAN ELEPHANT
To keep its skin in good condition, it needs to bathe frequently. All elephants are herbivores. Rare. S-E Asia. SH 3m max.

⬇ AFRICAN ELEPHANT
The largest land animal. Lives in herds with an old female in charge. Adult males live separately. Rare. Africa. SH 4m max.

Small ears and round back

Large ears

For a link to a virtual zoo where you can pet animals, turn to page 60.

DOLPHIN, SEALS

➡ BOTTLE-NOSED DOLPHIN
Like most dolphins, easily bored and may behave unnaturally in zoos as a result. Communicates with whistles and squeaks. Uses echo location to detect distant objects. World-wide.
H&B 3.6m max.

Breathes through its blowhole

Ear flaps

⬅ CALIFORNIAN SEALION
Swims by moving its fore-limbs. Its coat appears light fawn when it is dry. The males are called bulls, the females, cows. N Pacific coasts. H&B 2.3m.

Sealions turn their hind limbs forward when walking

➡ GREY SEAL
Seals are not as acrobatic on land as sealions. Try to time how long it stays under water (up to 15 minutes). Babies have white fur. N Atlantic coasts. H&B 3.1m max.

Seals' hind limbs are useless on land

No ear flaps

ZEBRAS, HORSE, TAPIR

➡ GRANT'S ZEBRA
Zebras have different rump patterns. **Grevy's Zebras** (rare) bray like donkeys; **Chapman's** and **Grant's** bark; **Mountain zebras** (rare) neigh. **All:** Africa. SH 1.1m.

Rump

Mountain zebra

Grevy's zebra

Chapman's zebra

Stiff mane

White muzzle

⬅ PRZEWALSKI'S HORSE/ TAKH
Pronounced "pshuh-vaal-ski". The only living wild horse, saved from extinction by breeding in zoos. Mongolia. SH 1.1m.

➡ MALAYAN TAPIR
Herbivore. Uses its long lips to pluck food. Feet are specialized for swampy ground and get sore on hard ground. Rare. S-E Asia. SH 1.1m.

17

For a link to the Worldwide Fund for Nature website, turn to page 60.

RHINOCEROS, HIPPOPOTAMUS

➡ INDIAN RHINOCEROS
Has only one horn. Herbivore browser. Rare. S Asia. SH 2m max.

➡ BLACK RHINOCEROS
Left Hide is dark grey. Rare. Africa. SH 1.7m max.

➡ WHITE RHINOCEROS
Right Hide is slate grey to yellowish brown. Large shoulder hump. Rare. Africa. SH 1.9m max.

Pointed upper lip for browsing

Square upper lip for grazing

⬅ HIPPOPOTAMUS
Spends most of the day in water. Can stay under water for up to 5 mins. Herbivore. Africa. SH 1.5m.

Large tusks inside mouth

⬅ PYGMY HIPPOPOTAMUS
Its skin secretes an oil that stops it drying out on land. Rare. W Africa. SH 1m.

PECCARY, CAMEL, LLAMA

➡ PECCARY

Not a true pig. If excited, hair over a scent gland near the tail base sticks up and you will smell a musky scent. The young are reddish with a black back-stripe. C & S America. SH 50cm.

Scent gland

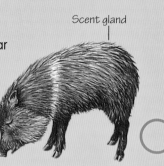

⬅ BACTRIAN CAMEL

A two-humped camel from Asia. The **dromedary** from Arabia has one hump. Both are used for riding and carrying loads. Humps store fat, which is used if there is no food. SH 1.8m.

Protective skin on the knees

Very mobile ears for good hearing

➡ LLAMA

Related to camels and, like them, may spit when angry. Its wild ancestor is the **guanaco**, like a slender llama with a red-brown coat. S America. SH 1.2m.

GIRAFFE, OKAPI

Both the male and female have horns, sometimes four or five.

➡ GIRAFFE
The world's tallest animal. Lips and long tongue used to pluck leaves. Gentle, but can give a nasty kick. Mostly silent, but can moo or grunt. Usually sleeps standing up. Africa.
SH 3.1m.
H&B 5m.

The lower jaw moves from side to side when the giraffe eats.

These are some of the other coat patterns you may see.

Due to its long neck, the giraffe must spread its front legs apart to stoop and drink.

⬅ OKAPI
The giraffe's only living relative, discovered in 1901. Its blue-black tongue is long enough to reach its ears. The male has tiny horns covered by skin. Rare. Congo region, Africa. SH 1.6m. H&B 1.9m.

♂

For a link to the US Wildlife Conservation Society's site, turn to page 60.

DEER

➡ PÈRE DAVID'S DEER
Extinct in the wild, now
only found in zoos. Has
a dark winter coat and
a light summer coat.
Lives in a large herd led
by a stag. Originally from
China. SH 1.1m.

The skin has
been rubbed off
these antlers.

Summer
coat

♂

Both sexes
have antlers

♂

← REINDEER
Like all deer, it sheds
its antlers each year.
New ones are covered
with velvety skin, which is
eventually rubbed off. Eats
lichen. Arctic. SH 1.3m.

Broad hooves
for walking on
snow

Antlers

♂

➡ REEVES' MUNTJAC
Male has small antlers.
Holds its head low when
running. Barks when alarmed.
China. (Escaped animals
wild in S England). SH 50cm.

21

For a link to a gallery of the world's vanishing animals, turn to page 60.

ANTELOPES

➡ COMMON ORYX/ GEMSBOK
Like all antelopes, it never
sheds its horns. Africa.
SH 1.2m.

➡ SCIMITAR-HORNED ORYX
Believed to be extinct
in the wild. Sahara,
N Africa. SH 1m.

Both sexes
have horns

**⬅ WHITE-BEARDED
BRINDLED GNU/
BLUE WILDEBEEST**
Often live in huge herds
which migrate long
distances to find new
pasture. Active day
and night. Africa.
SH 1.2m.

➡ BLACKBUCK
Each herd has
one male
leader. Females
are nervous and
alert the herd
to danger.
S Asia.
SH 80cm.

22

For a link to photos and videos of endangered animals, turn to page 60.

ANTELOPES, BISON

➡ BLUE DUIKER
Small, shy antelope. Rubs
glands under its eyes
against objects to mark
out its territory. Africa.
SH 40cm.

Gland

Small hump

⬅ GREATER KUDU
The female is smaller
than the male and has
no horns or fringe on
the throat. Mainly a
browser. Africa.
SH 1.6m max.

♂

Large shoulder
hump

**➡ AMERICAN
BISON/ "BUFFALO"**
Bellows when angry.
Heavy, but can
move fast. Likes
rolling in mud and
dust. Rare. N America.
SH 2m max.

For a link to a "danger list" of the rarest mammals, turn to page 60.

OX, SAIGA, SHEEP, GOAT

➡ MUSK OX
Under its coarse
hair is a fine, woolly
undercoat. A herd will
stand in a line or circle
to face an attacker.
Rare. Arctic. SH 1.3m.

*Large,
wide feet*

Summer coat ♂

⬅ SAIGA
The male has horns and an
inflatable nose. The winter
coat is white and shaggy.
S Russia. SH 70cm.

➡ BARBARY SHEEP
The only sheep with
a throat-fringe. Both sexes
have horns. N Africa. SH 1m.

♂

Fringe

*Both sexes
have horns*

♂

*All goats
have beards*

⬅ MARKHOR
The largest wild goat.
Lives in herds usually led
by an old female. Rare.
Himalayas, Asia. SH 1m.

AUSTRALIAN POUCHED MAMMALS

➡ LONG-NOSED POTOROO
Related to the kangaroo.
Builds nests, carrying nest
material with its tail.
Nocturnal. Australia.
H&B 40cm.

⬅ WESTERN GREY KANGAROO
Powerful back legs. Can jump a 2m
fence. Like all Australian pouched
mammals, its young are born tiny and
naked. They climb up to the pouch and
develop inside it. Australia. H&B 1.5m.

⬇ RED KANGAROO
Has white face marks
and a pale tail tip.
Australia. H&B 1.5m.

Female is
usually grey.

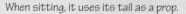

When sitting, it uses its tail as a prop.

➡ COMMON WOMBAT
Loves digging. Partly nocturnal,
it spends most of the day in its
burrow. Its pouch opens
backwards to keep out
soil. Australia. H&B 1.2m.

RODENTS

➡ CANADIAN BEAVER

The family lives in a "lodge" built of sticks and mud, with an underwater entrance. The main chamber is above water. N America. H&B 1m.

Slaps the water with its tail as an alarm signal

⬅ MARA

Related to the Guinea Pig. When moving quickly, it may hop like a rabbit. Lives in big groups which dig large burrows. S America. H&B 70cm.

Unlike most rodents, the Mara walks on its toes.

➡ BLACK-TAILED PRAIRIE DOG

Ground-living squirrel. Lives in big groups which dig burrows. A group of burrows is called a "town". N America. H&B 30cm.

Long claws used for digging

⬅ SIBERIAN CHIPMUNK

Ground-living squirrel. Very active. Carries food in its large cheek pouches. N Europe; Asia. H&B 10cm.

For a link to a website with games about conservation, turn to page 61.

WOLF, JACKAL, HUNTING DOG, FOX

➡ **GREY WOLF**
Group howling helps
attachments form
between all the pack
members, and warns other
packs of their presence.
Europe; N America; Asia.
H&B 1.2m max.

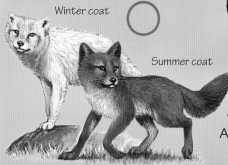

⬅ **BLACK-BACKED JACKAL**
Lives in pairs. Nocturnal
and shy. S & E Africa.
H&B 90cm max.

➡ **AFRICAN
HUNTING DOG**
Has a strange, hooting
call. Lives in groups with
a very strict social order.
Africa. H&B 1.1m max.

Very
strong
jaws

Winter coat

Summer coat

⬅ **ARCTIC FOX**
Its thick white winter
coat keeps it warm,
and makes it hard
to see in the snow.
Arctic. H&B 78cm max.

27

HYENA, COATI, MEERKAT, OTTER

➡ SPOTTED/ LAUGHING HYENA

Lives in groups. A powerful predator and scavenger. It "laughs" at mating time. Africa. H&B 85cm.

Strong jaws used to crunch bone

➡ RING-TAILED COATI

Adult females live in groups. Intelligent and skilful with their claws. C & S America. H&B 65cm max.

Always sniffing things with its flexible nose

Uses its tail to balance when climbing

⬅ MEERKAT/ SURICATE

A type of mongoose. Lives in big groups in burrows. "Guards" sit upright to look for danger while the pack is feeding. S Africa. H&B 30cm.

⬅ CANADIAN OTTER

Partly nocturnal. Loves acrobatics in water, but also spends much time on land. N America. H&B 1m.

Uses its tail as a rudder when swimming

For a link to the website of London Zoo, turn to page 61.

BEARS

➡ ASIATIC BLACK BEAR
Dangerous, like all bears, killing with one swipe of its paw. Omnivore. C & E Asia. The **American Black Bear** has no white V on its chest. Omnivore. H&B 1.6m max.

Standing on two legs is a threatening sign

Long claws

⬅ BROWN BEAR
Walks on the soles of its feet, like all bears. Large shoulder hump. The **American Grizzly's** fur is often pale at the tips. Europe, Asia. H&B 3m max.

➡ POLAR BEAR
A powerful hunter in the wild. Thick fur and a fat layer beneath its skin keep it warm enough to swim safely in the freezing waters of the Arctic. Rare. Arctic. H&B 2.5m.

The feet have hairy soles.

29

For a link to the latest news from Barcelona Zoo, turn to page 61.

BEAR, PANDAS

➡ SUN BEAR
A tropical bear which needs a lot of warmth. Nests in trees. Laps up termites with its long tongue. Especially loves wild honey. Omnivore. S-E Asia. H&B 1.4m max.

U-shaped chest marking

Naked soles

⬅ GIANT PANDA
Once thought the closest relative of the Red Panda, it is now classed as a bear. Tends to live alone. Has special pads on its hands to help it grip bamboo, which is its main diet. Scent-marks its territory by rubbing its bottom on the ground. Rare. China. H&B 1.5m.

Bamboo

➡ RED PANDA
Related to the raccoons. Eats bamboo like the Giant Panda. Rare. Himalayas. H&B 65cm max.

CATS

➡ SERVAL
Runs very quickly over short distances, but climbs little. Has a repetitive, yowling cry. Its hearing is acute. Africa. H&B 95cm.

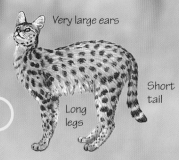

Very large ears

Short tail

Long legs

Bushy tail

⬅ WILD CAT
Looks like a domestic cat, but is larger and stronger. Has a broad head and a bushy tail. Mainly nocturnal. Europe, Africa, W Asia. H&B 60cm.

➡ OCELOT
Like all cats, it scent-marks its territory with urine. Ocelots are an endangered species due to being hunted for their beautiful fur. Rare. C & S America. H&B 1.3m.

⬅ JUNGLE CAT
Can climb, but spends most of its time on the ground. Like most cats, it can retract its claws. This stops them getting blunt. S Asia. H&B 60cm.

31

For a link to a photo gallery of animals in the Bronx Zoo, turn to page 61.

CATS

➡ PUMA/ COUGAR/ MOUNTAIN LION

Usually silent, but yowls and screams at mating time. Kittens have spots on their backs and sides. N & S America. H&B 2m max.

Ear tufts

Winter coat

⬅ NORTHERN LYNX

Hisses when angry, and two tufts of fur on its throat stick out. In the wild, it grows a thick winter coat. N America; N Europe; N Asia. H&B 1.3m max.

Ear tufts

Short tail

➡ CARACAL

Lives alone. Jumps and climbs very well. The ear tufts are believed to be used for signalling. Mainly nocturnal. Africa; W Asia. H&B 70cm.

Very long, thick tail

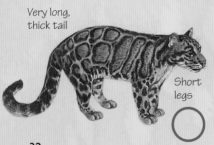

Short legs

⬅ CLOUDED LEOPARD

An excellent climber, it can hang upside-down from branches by its hind feet. Nocturnal. Rare. S-E Asia. H&B 95cm.

Thick winter coat

➡ SNOW LEOPARD
Purrs, but does not roar. On cold nights, it wraps its long tail around its body to keep its head and nose warm. Rare. C Asia. H&B 1m.

Rosette spots

⬅ LEOPARD
Can leap great distances. Usually silent, but may make a coughing noise. Africa; Asia. H&B 1.5m.

⬇ BLACK PANTHER
A dark-brown form of the leopard. Africa; Asia. H&B 1.5m.

The spots are still visible

There are black spots inside the rosettes

➡ JAGUAR
Not a fast runner, but an excellent swimmer. It lives near rivers, preying on animals that come to drink. There are also black jaguars. C & S America. H&B 1.8m.

Short legs

33

For a link to the San Diego Zoo website, turn to page 61.

CATS

➡ LION

Unlike all other cats, it lives in big groups, called "prides". Most of the time it rests. The females do most of the hunting. Africa; S-W Asia.
H&B 2.5m max.

Female has no mane

♂

⬅ TIGER

The largest cat. Lives alone. Swims very well. There are several races (permanent varieties) varying in colour and size. The **White Tiger**, for example has white fur with stripes. Very rare. Asia. H&B 3m max.

➡ CHEETAH

The fastest land animal over short distances. It can reach speeds of 110 kph. The cubs have a silver mane down their backs. Rare. Africa. H&B 2m max.

Can only retract its claws partially

34

For a link to online adventures about tiger survival, turn to page 61.

FLIGHTLESS BIRDS

➡ EMU
Has "hairy" feathers. Like
the Cassowary, the male
Emu keeps the eggs
warm and rears the
young without help
from the female.
Australia.
TL 2m.

Three
toes

♂

♀

Unlike other
birds, it has
only two
toes

⬅ OSTRICH
The largest bird. Runs
very fast on its long,
powerful legs. A male
lives with several
females, which lay
eggs in the same nest.
It is usually the male
that keeps the eggs
warm. Africa. TL 2.4m.

**➡ AUSTRALIAN
CASSOWARY**
One of its three toes has
a long, dagger-like claw,
which it uses for fighting.
It usually lives alone.
Australia. TL 1.5m.

Three
toes

Fighting
claw

FLAMINGOS, GOOSE

➡ GREATER FLAMINGO
All flamingos live in large groups. They feed by holding their heads upside-down and sifting water through their bills. Asia; Mediterranean. TL 1.4m.

⬇ LESSER FLAMINGO
The smallest flamingo. Varies from pale to dark pink. E Africa. TL 1m.

Lots of
black
on bill

➡ CHILEAN FLAMINGO
Left Pale pink. All flamingo chicks are white or grey. S America. TL 1m.

➡ CARIBBEAN/ ROSY FLAMINGO
Right Deep pink or red. Caribbean coasts; Galapagos Islands. TL 1.2m.

⬅ NÉ NÉ/ HAWAIIAN GOOSE
Nearly became extinct, but zoo-bred birds are now being released into the wild. Hawaii. TL 73cm max.

PENGUINS, DUCK, IBIS

➡ KING PENGUIN
Males and females take turns to incubate eggs. Penguins cannot fly, but swim superbly. Antarctic. TL 94cm.

➡ AFRICAN/ JACKASS PENGUIN
Makes a braying, croaking noise. Sub-Antarctic; S African coast. TL 72cm.

➡ ROCKHOPPER PENGUIN
As its name implies, it moves by hopping between rocks. Antarctic & Sub-Antarctic. TL 56cm.

"Sail" feathers are lost in summer

♂

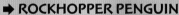

⬅ MANDARIN DUCK
The male uses his bright colours and "sail" feathers to court the dull-brown female. They perch and nest in trees. China. TL 43cm.

➡ SCARLET IBIS
Like many birds, it often washes bits of food in its drinking water before eating. S America. TL 58cm.

Beak turns black in the breeding season

CRANE, STORK, PELICAN

➡ CROWNED CRANE
In spring, watch for their
courtship dance. Both
sexes flap their wings and
leap into the air with loud
cries. They may pair for
life. They mainly eat small
mammals, such as mice.
E Africa. TL 1.1m.

Function of the
neck pouch is
unknown

⬅ MARABOU STORK
One of the largest storks.
Usually silent, but like
most storks, it rattles its
bill loudly when courting.
In the wild it eats carrion
(dead meat). Africa.
TL 1.3m.

Skin
pouch

**➡ EUROPEAN
WHITE PELICAN**
Lives in large groups.
Uses its bill and skin pouch
as a scoop for catching fish.
Waddles on land, but can
swim and fly well. E Europe;
Asia; S Africa. TL 1.5m.

Webbed
feet. Four
forward-
facing toes.

PHEASANTS, GUINEAFOWL

➡ INDIAN PEAFOWL
A type of pheasant.
Only the male
(peacock) has long
feathers. He fans them
out and shakes them
when courting the
female (peahen).
India. TL 2m.

➡ GOLDEN PHEASANT
The male displays to
the brown female by
spreading his ruff
feathers and golden
wings. W China.
TL 1m.

Pheasants lose their
long "covert" feathers
(see below) after the
mating season.

◀ LADY AMHERST'S PHEASANT
As with all pheasants, what looks
like the tail is really a collection of
long "covert" feathers. The true
tail is hidden beneath them.
China. TL 1.5m.

➡ HELMETED GUINEAFOWL
Listen for its noisy, metallic
cry. Africa. TL 55cm.

OWLS, CARACARA

Female is slightly larger than the male ♀

♂

➡ SNOWY OWL
Unlike most owls, it is active during the day. Its white feathers camouflage it against the Arctic snows. Arctic. TL 56cm.

➡ SPECTACLED OWL
Lives near water. The young are white with a black "mask". C & S America. TL 45cm.

Feather-tufts

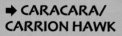

⬅ EURASIAN EAGLE OWL
A large owl. Its feather-tufts are not ears. They help owls recognize each other. Flies quietly, like all owls. Europe; N Africa; Asia. TL 71cm max.

➡ CARACARA/ CARRION HAWK
Its strong beak and claws are used for tearing dead meat. S America. TL 55cm.

For a link to the website of the UK's RSPB, turn to page 60.

EAGLES

➡ EUROPEAN GOLDEN EAGLE

Like most birds of prey, the female is larger than the male. Mating pairs stay together for life. Prey is caught with powerful claws and carried off for eating. Europe. TL 78cm.

Colour and size vary with habitat and age

Hooked beak

⬅ AFRICAN FISH EAGLE

Dives from treetops to catch fish. Like most birds of prey, it has excellent vision. It throws back its head when making its distinctive, screeching call. Africa. TL 74cm.

Very long, pointed wings

➡ BATELEUR EAGLE

When hunting in the wild, it can glide for hours on its long wings. Has a spectacular courtship display in the air. Africa. TL 64cm.

Short tail

41

For a link to facts about the animals in Toronto Zoo, turn to page 61.

VULTURES, CONDOR

➡ GRIFFON VULTURE
Vultures feed on carrion (dead meat). They have bald heads, as feathers would get matted with blood during feeding.
Europe; S-W Asia; S Africa. TL 1.1m max.

Hooked beak used for tearing meat

⬅ KING VULTURE
Like all New World vultures, both sexes circle each other, during courtship, whistling and flapping their wings. Unlike many birds, it is believed to use its sense of smell to find food.
C & S America. TL 80cm.

Comb

Wattles

Female has no comb or wattles

➡ ANDEAN CONDOR
Stretches out its wings to warm them in the sun.
Wingspan of over 3m.
Female has red eyes.
S America. TL 1.3m max.

42

For a link to the website of Victoria's Three Zoos, turn to page 61.

PARROTS

➡ SULPHUR-CRESTED COCKATOO

Screams when excited. May live in large flocks in the wild. Both sexes have crests, and raise them as signals – especially the male at mating time. Australia. TL 50cm.

Crest

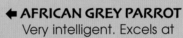

⬅ AFRICAN GREY PARROT

Very intelligent. Excels at mimicking voices. Long-lived, like most parrots, often reaching 50 years. Lives in large flocks in the wild. C & W Africa. TL 33cm.

➡ BLUE AND YELLOW MACAW

Left S America. TL 86cm.

➡ SCARLET MACAW

Right C & S America. TL 85cm. All macaws grip hard fruit and nuts with their claws and peel them, or crack them open, with their strong, hooked beaks. They nest in the hollows of trees.

43

PARROTS

➡ YELLOW-BACKED LORY
Like most parrots, it nests in
tree-holes. Lories differ from
Lorikeets in having short tails.
Moluccas, Indonesia.
TL 30cm.

⬅ RAINBOW LORIKEET
Its special tongue helps it to eat
pollen and nectar. It also eats
fruit, leaves, etc. Very noisy.
Australasia. TL 26cm.

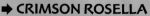

➡ CRIMSON ROSELLA
Eats mainly seeds.
Spends a lot of time
on the ground. S & E
Australia. TL 36cm.

⬅ FISCHER'S LOVEBIRD
Pairs of lovebirds sit closely
together. They groom
each other a lot. In the
wild they live in flocks.
E Africa. TL 15cm.

44

TOUCANS, TURACO, MINAH, HORNBILL

➤ ARIEL TOUCAN
Orange beak

➤ SULPHUR-BREASTED TOUCAN
Green beak
Large, lightweight beaks help toucans pick fruit off trees. S America. TL 52cm.

Crest—

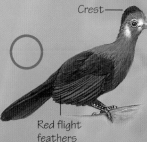

Red flight feathers

◄ WHITE-CHEEKED TURACO
Dips as it flies. Has strong feet for jumping and running along branches. W Africa. TL 42cm.

Lightweight beak and horny casque

➤ GREAT INDIAN HORNBILL
At nesting time, the female walls herself into a hole, leaving a slit through which the male feeds her. S-E Asia. TL 1.2m.

◄ NEPAL HILL MINAH
Can mimic voices well. Becomes aggressive at nesting time. S-E Asia. TL 31cm.

ROLLER, PIGEON, MOTMOT, KOOKABURRA

➡ LILAC-BREASTED ROLLER
Named for its rolling, wheeling flight. Mates in the air. Hunts from a perch, taking the food back to the same perch. Africa. TL 36cm.

➡ BLUE-CROWNED PIGEON
Largest pigeon in the world. Feeds on the ground, but flies off if alarmed. New Guinea. TL 68cm.

Saw-edged beak

⬅ BLUE-CROWNED MOTMOT
Sits for long periods on its perch. Central parts of its tail feathers are worn bare from preening and rubbing against objects. C & S America. TL 45cm.

The upper side of the tail is blue

➡ KOOKABURRA/ LAUGHING JACKASS
Cackling call. Kills small prey by banging them against a branch. Australia. TL 46cm.

WHYDAH, STARLING, FINCHES

➡ PARADISE WHYDAH

Lays eggs in the nests of other birds. The male has two long tail feathers in the breeding season. Africa. TL 40cm.

♂ Breeding plumage

➡ PURPLE GLOSSY STARLING

Noisy and aggressive. All starlings are good at mimicking sounds. They sometimes mimic other birds. Africa. TL 22cm.

♂

⬅ GOULDIAN FINCH

There are several different colour patterns. Like other grass-finches, both sexes help to keep the eggs warm. Australia. TL 14cm.

➡ BLACK-HEADED WEAVER

Nests in groups, each pair building a nest woven from grass, suspended from a branch. W Africa. TL 15cm.

♂

Entrance

CONSTRICTING SNAKES

➡ ANACONDA
Non-poisonous. Spends a lot of time in water. All the snakes on this page are **constrictors** – they suffocate their prey. S America. TL 11.5m max.

Snakes have no outer ear parts

⬅ BOA CONSTRICTOR
Non-poisonous. Can climb. Its tail is slightly prehensile. Mainly nocturnal. C & S America. TL 5.5m max.

All constrictors can open their mouths very wide to swallow large prey

➡ INDIAN PYTHON
There are about 20 python species. All non-poisonous. They lay eggs (anacondas and boas bear live young). S-E Asia. TL 7.6m max. **African python**. TL 5.5m max. **Reticulated python**. S-E Asia. TL 10m max. **Royal/Ball python**. Curls into a ball if frightened. W Africa. TL 1.3m max. **Carpet python**. New Guinea; Australia. TL 4.3m max.

African python

Royal python

Reticulated python

Carpet python

48

For a link to the latest news from Auckland Zoo, turn to page 61.

POISONOUS SNAKES

➡ GREEN MAMBA
Lives in branches. Moves quickly.
Like all snakes, it swallows its prey
whole. Lays eggs. Africa. TL 2.4m max.

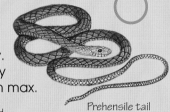

Prehensile tail

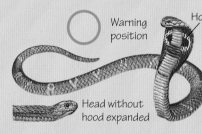

Warning position

Hood

Head without hood expanded

⬅ INDIAN COBRA
If frightened, its neck
ribs move, expanding
the skin to form a hood.
It may then strike.
S Asia. TL 1.8m max.

➡ PUFF ADDER
A viper. If frightened,
it puffs up to look
threatening. All vipers bear
live young. Africa. TL 90cm.

All vipers hiss when frightened

➡ GABOON VIPER
Strikes from a coiled
position. Long front
fangs are folded
back until it actually
strikes. Africa. TL 1.2m.

Rattle

⬅ EASTERN DIAMONDBACK RATTLESNAKE
Shakes "rattle" on the
end of its tail to give a
warning. E USA. TL 1.5m.

49

For a link to a site where you can play wildlife games, turn to page 61.

LIZARDS

➡ COMMON IGUANA

Has sharp claws and climbs well. Will lash out at an enemy with its long, powerful tail. C & S America. TL 1.3m max.

➡ COMMON CHAMELEON

Skin colour changes if it is excited, or if the light or temperature alter. Mediterranean. TL 30cm max.

Prehensile tail

Shoots out a long, sticky tongue to catch insects

⬅ STUMPY-TAILED/ SHINGLEBACK SKINK

Slow mover. Lives in the desert. Stores fat in its tail, like many desert reptiles. Australia. TL 45cm max.

➡ LEOPARD GECKO

Fast mover. Climbs well using special gripping pads on its feet. S Asia. TL 30cm max.

Lashes its tail when angry

⬅ NILE MONITOR

Good swimmer. Sharp claws for climbing, digging and defence. Tears its food with sharp teeth. Africa. TL 1.8m.

CROCODILE, ALLIGATOR, TURTLE, TORTOISE

➡ NILE CROCODILE
Keeps very still most of the time, but can move quickly. Can stay under water for over an hour. Africa. TL 5m max.

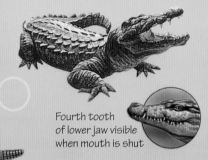

Fourth tooth of lower jaw visible when mouth is shut

⬅ AMERICAN ALLIGATOR
Has a broader snout than a crocodile. Eggs laid in large mound-shaped mud nests. The young are black with yellow markings. S-E USA. TL 6m max.

➡ HAWKSBILL TURTLE
Eats sponges. Leaves the ocean to lay eggs. Very rare. Tropical oceans. SL 91cm max.

Beak-like mouth

⬅ GIANT TORTOISE
May live to a great age. Very rare. Galapagos Islands, Pacific Ocean. SL 1.5m max.

NOCTURNAL ANIMALS

➡ SENEGAL BUSHBABY/ GALAGO
Has finger-pads to grip branches.
Strong back legs. Can leap over
2m upwards. Africa. H&B 17cm.

Ears can move
separately or
be folded back

Superb
night vision

⬅ TARSIER
Like an owl, it can hardly
move its huge eyes, but
can turn its head to
look over its shoulder.
S-E Asia. H&B
12.5cm.

➡ COLUGO/ FLYING LEMUR
Not a lemur, but in an order of
its own. It glides between the
rainforest trees on its special
skin-flaps. S-E Asia.
H&B 37.5cm.

Sharp claws help
it to climb

**⬇ LARGE FRUIT BAT/
MALAYAN FLYING FOX**
Unlike most bats, fruit bats have no echo-
location sense. Has acute hearing and
eyesight, but cannot fly in total darkness.
S-E Asia. H&B 40cm. Wingspan 2m max.

➡ NAKED MOLE RAT
Hardly any hair. Sensitive whiskers
on snout. Long front teeth used for
tunnelling. Lives in underground colonies
with a strict social order. One female
and up to three males are involved
in mating. E Africa. H&B 10.4cm.

No ear-
flaps

➡ JERBOA
Lives in deserts. Its hind legs are
much longer than its front legs.
Can cover 3m in one bound.
Gets all the water it needs
from eating roots and seeds.
N Africa; Asia. H&B 15cm max.

Long tail
aids balance

⬇ KANGAROO RAT
Like the jerboa, it lives in deserts, moves
by hopping, and needs little water. Acute
hearing. Camouflaged well in the desert
by its sandy coloration. Stores
food in cheek pouches.
N America. H&B 16cm max.

White
stripe on
hips

➡ NORTH AMERICAN
PORCUPINE
A rodent, like all the animals
on this page. If attacked, it
will turn around and thrust
the long quills on its back into
the predator. Herbivore.
H&B 1m max.

NOCTURNAL ANIMALS

➡ FENNEC FOX
Lives in deserts. Its large ears lose heat to keep it cool. Acute hearing. Rests in a burrow during the day. N Africa; Sinai; Arabia. H&B 38.5cm.

⬅ DINGO
Believed to descend from dogs brought to Australia by Aboriginal settlers. Has short, soft, yellowish to reddish-brown hair. It yelps and howls, but does not usually bark. Australia. H&B 90cm.

➡ NORTH AMERICAN RACCOON
Lives in woods, but will enter towns to seek food. Likes to wash its food. Climbs and swims well. Omnivore. N & C America. H&B 57.5cm.

Nimble, hand-like forepaws

Tail raised as a threat

⬅ STRIPED SKUNK
Raises its tail to warn predators away. If this fails, it releases a foul smell from a scent gland under its tail. N America. H&B 38.5cm.

➡ INDIAN/GREY MONGOOSE

Brave. Kills and eats cobras. Not immune to their venom, but very agile, and can resist several bites. Asia; Arabia. H&B 30cm.

Thick, protective fur

➡ AARDVARK

No front teeth. Laps up termites with its sticky 40cm tongue. Spends the day in a burrow. Coat varies from sparse and sandy to full, glossy black. C & S Africa. H&B 1.2m max.

Large claws used to break into termite mounds

⬅ PANGOLIN/SCALY ANTEATER

Greenish scales made of modified hair. Uses claws and tongue, like the aardvark, to hunt termites, but is toothless. Rolls into a ball if threatened. Some pangolin species live in trees. Africa; S-E Asia. H&B 90cm max.

➡ ECHIDNA/SPINY ANTEATER

Lays an egg, which is kept in a pouch. In danger, it burrows down, leaving only its spikes showing. Australia; New Guinea. H&B 78cm max.

55

For a link to a website with the latest animal news, turn to page 61.

NOCTURNAL ANIMALS

➜ KOALA
It gets all the water it
needs from its sole
diet of eucalyptus
leaves. Carries young
in a pouch. When
older, the young
travel by gripping
their parent's back.
Australia. H&B 78.5cm.

← BOODIE
A type of Rat Kangaroo. Carries
young in a pouch. Eats fruit, bulbs and
seeds. W Australia. Rare. H&B 28cm.

➜ BROWN KIWI
The only bird with nostrils
that open at the tip of its beak.
Used to sniff out worms under the soil.
Its egg is huge in relation to its body.
Flightless. New Zealand. TL 50cm.

Black and white pattern
camouflages it against
the forest canopy.

← SPOTTED LINSANG
Tree-dwelling. Like a cat, it
pounces on its prey and can retract
its claws. Feeds on insects, birds and
small mammals. S Asia. H&B 38cm.

56

For a link to a site with tips on taking photos at the zoo, turn to page 61.

VERY RARE ANIMALS

A number of the animals in this book, such as the Tiger, are rare in the wild. Sometimes they are few because of competition with other animals, but more often it is due to hunting by humans, or destruction of their habitat as human industry grows. Many of the animals in this section are so rare you may not see them, even in a zoo.

➡ EASTERN QUOLL
Pouched Australian mammal. Female may have up to 30 young in a litter. Only six usually survive. S-E Australia. H&B 45cm max.

Large ears give acute hearing

⬅ BILBY/ RABBIT-EARED BANDICOOT
Lives in a burrow during the day. Young are carried in a backward-opening pouch. Australia. H&B 55cm max.

➡ GIANT ARMADILLO
Related to anteaters and sloths. Feeds on termites. Its bony plates form a flexible shell. Balances on its hind legs and tail to reach the tops of termite mounds. C & S America. H&B 1m max.

Large claws for burrowing, and breaking into termite mounds

VERY RARE ANIMALS

➡ CARIBBEAN MANATEE
No hind legs. Lives in both fresh
and sea water. Active day and
night. Herbivore. Coasts
of Caribbean, E Mexico
& S-E USA. H&B 3.25m.

⬅ GOLDEN LION TAMARIN
Uses its long, clawed fingers
to dig insects out of cracks in
bark. Lives in family groups.
All members help to care
for the young. Omnivore.
S-E Brazil. H&B 36.6cm max.

➡ HYACINTH MACAW
The largest parrot. Lives in
large flocks. Cracks open palm
nuts with its powerful beak.
The beak is also used to aid
climbing. S America. TL 1m.

⬇ KAKAPO
The rarest and heaviest parrot.
A nocturnal, flightless, solitary
herbivore. To attract
mates, males gather
in hollows, inflate their
chests and boom loudly.
New Zealand.
TL 60cm max.

WORLD MAP

KEY TO MAP

North America
| | USA |
| | Mexico |

South America
| | Brazil |

Europe
| | England |
| | Russia |

Africa
| | Ethiopia |
| | Madagascar |

Asia
	China
	Mongolia
	India
	Malaysia
	Indonesia

Australasia
| | Australia |
| | New Zealand |

① Caribbean Sea
② Mediterranean Sea
③ Sahara Desert
④ Congo Region
⑤ Sinai
⑥ Arabia
⑦ Himalayas

These geographical regions are used in this book:

Sub-Antarctic The area immediately surrounding the Antarctic circle.

Tropical The warm region between the Tropics of Cancer and Capricorn.

Sub-tropical The area immediately surrounding the Tropical region.

59

For a link to games about wildlife around the world, turn to page 61.

INTERNET LINKS

If you have access to the Internet, you can visit these websites to find out more about wild animals. For links to these sites, go to the Usborne Quicklinks Website at **www.usborne-quicklinks.com** and enter the keywords "spotters wild animals".

Internet safety

When using the Internet, please follow the **Internet safety guidelines** shown on the Usborne Quicklinks Website.

ANIMALS OF THE WORLD

WEBSITE 1   Find your favourite animal in an online encyclopedia.

WEBSITE 2   Pictures, videos, sounds and games on a wide range of animals.

WEBSITE 3   Find fast facts about animals, and watch videos and webcams.

WEBSITE 4   Animal fact files, with photos, fun facts and video and audio clips.

WEBSITE 5   Visit a virtual zoo and pet animals online.

ENDANGERED ANIMALS AND CONSERVATION

WEBSITE 1   Learn about the global efforts of the Worldwide Fund for Nature.

WEBSITE 2   Find out about the work of the UK's Royal Society for the Protection of Birds (RSPB).

WEBSITE 3   Discover the US Wildlife Conservation Society's activities worldwide.

WEBSITE 4   View a picture gallery of the world's vanishing animals.

WEBSITE 5   See photos and video clips of Earth's endangered animals.

WEBSITE 6   Read a "danger list" of the world's rarest mammals.

WEBSITE 7 Play games to find out more about conservation.

ZOOS AND WILDLIFE PARKS WORLDWIDE

WEBSITE 1 London Zoo (UK) – meet some of the animals online.

WEBSITE 2 Barcelona Zoo (Spain) – read the latest news and visit a virtual zoo.

WEBSITE 3 Bronx Zoo (USA) – browse a photo gallery of animals.

WEBSITE 4 San Diego Zoo and Wild Animal Park (USA) – watch videos and read the latest zoo newsletter.

WEBSITE 5 Toronto Zoo (Canada) – find out facts about the zoo's animals.

WEBSITE 6 Victoria's Three Zoos (Australia) – read about the animals that live there.

WEBSITE 7 Auckland Zoo (New Zealand) – catch up with all the latest zoo news.

ANIMAL FUN

WEBSITE 1 Try some online adventures about helping tigers to survive.

WEBSITE 2 Play wildlife games.

WEBSITE 3 Read the latest animal news and stories.

WEBSITE 4 Play games and quizzes about wildlife around the world.

WEBSITE 5 A website with helpful tips for taking great photos at the zoo.

USEFUL WORDS

browser – an animal that eats mainly the leaves of trees and bushes.

canine teeth – long, sharp teeth at each side of the jaws, used to seize prey.

carnivores – meat-eaters.

Carnivora – an order of mammals, such as lions, with teeth specialized for eating flesh.

class – an animal group within a phylum, for example, the mammals.

conservation – the efforts made to protect nature in order to safeguard the future of all living things.

echo location – the ability of animals such as bats to locate objects by detecting echoes bouncing off them.

family – an animal group within an order, such as the *Felidae* (Cats).

genus – an animal group within a family, such as *Panthera* (Big Cats).

grazer – an animal that eats mainly grasses.

grooming – animals keeping themselves, or each other, clean by licking, or picking off insects.

habitat – the area in which an animal naturally lives.

herbivores – plant-eaters.

mammals – a class of hairy, warm-blooded animals that suckle their young with milk.

marsupials – a group of mammals that suckle their young in a pouch.

omnivores – animals that eat both plants and meat.

order – an animal group within a class, for example, the *Carnivora*.

phylum – any of the largest divisions of the Animal Kingdom.

prehensile – a term that describes a body part specialized for grasping, such as an elephant's trunk.

rodents (*Rodentia*) – an order of mammals, such as mice, with chisel-shaped front teeth specialized for gnawing.

scent gland – an organ that releases scent, often as a signal to other animals.

species – a specific type of animal within a genus, such as the tiger.

territory – the part of an animal's habitat that it defends as its own.

INDEX